T0132081

Expressions of Milk

A Poetry Collection for Mothers

Juhi Kunde

Illustrated by Cathie Lowmiller

To order additional copies of this book, contact:
Xlibris
1-888-795-4274
www.Xlibris.com
Orders@Xlibris.com

For mothers,

the expecting and the experienced,
the fresh and the fatigued,
the cautious and the carefree.

With empathy and gratitude,
Juhi and Cathie

Milk, like motherhood, has many forms—the exciting beginnings of fresh milk, the frustrations of spilled milk, the joys of ice cream, and the aging of cheese.

Contents

Fresh Milk

Expressions of New Beginnings

Impact

Your first shoes are
your first imprint on the world,
                    they say.
Your first indentation,
                    they say.
As usual,

                    they are
                    wrong.

Your first impact was
        so heavy the boulders squished
                so bright, the rainbows exploded
                        so loud, the avalanches faltered.

You looked at me
with newborn eyes,
and the universe shifted.

Now two moons hang in the sky.

Potential

Our little seed is planted in the ground.
Water and minerals, yes,
sun and care, yes,
but faith of a world beyond is truly what pushes it to be
visible, tangible, living.

Once birthed into the air,
our little plant fights
to breathe, yes,
to grow, yes,
but truly it dreams of bursting with color—
vibrant, exotic, thriving.

Mutual Comfort

The thick rubbery rope,
a bridge
pulsing with life juice.

My secret fears flow, wild and vicious, to you—
    untamed, raging fires,
        screaming and twisting nightmares
            of pain inconceivable conceived.

But you soothe them
    with your dances and hiccups,
        hopes of pillow fights
            and caramel sundaes.

Waking with the tickles
of your silent giggles,

I sing us back to sleep.

Baby's Dreamscape

One, two, buckle my shoe;
Three blind mice, see how they run—they all ran after the farmer's;
Wife takes the child, hi-ho-the-derry-o, the wife takes the child.

Little Ms. Muffet sat on a tuffet, eating her curds and whey;
Along came a spider, went up the waterspout—down came the rain.
Rain, go away, come again another day.

Little Jack Horner sat
On a wall, Humpty Dumpty had a great fall;
Down and broke his crown,
And Jill jumped over the moon.

First Hours as a Family

Blue pills, water,
Woozy, drowsy,
Grasping for my glasses.

Is she breathing? Is she yellow?
Is she breathing? Is she hungry?
Is she breathing?

A pixie in a sterile bassinet,
Healing emergency, cesarean.

Is she breathing? Can she hear?
Is she breathing? Will she love me?
Is she breathing?

Nurse Nancy demands a name.
Not Nancy.
Where are my glasses?

Is she breathing? Will she nurse?
Is she breathing? Will she be happy?
Is she breathing?

Broad hands surround her fragile
body.
Relieved and exhausted, I weep.
Her daddy promises to hold her
So I can get some sleep.

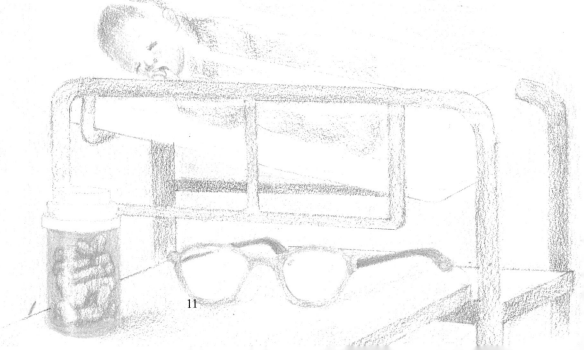

Spilled Milk

Expressions of Fatigue and Frustration

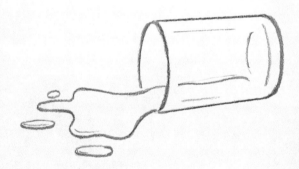

Quiet Time

Saturday morning,
stretch and yawn,
tiptoe through the house at dawn,
hurrying downstairs to relax.

A sparrow sings softly outside.
He swoops off his branch,
enjoying the ride.

The coffeepot drips
a muted *splot*, *splot*, *splot*;
hurry up, I need to relax.

Cotton-soled slippers warm my toes;
I pace in the kitchen.
An anxious knot grows.
Hurry—it's my time to relax!

My mug waits with sugar and milk,
a finger tapping its side—*splot*, *splot*,
splot.
When there's enough for half a cup,
my hand darts for the big black pot.

A quick stir and I'm off
to the couch:

Kick off slippers.
Tuck feet under.
Ready.

Savor
         the
                  silence.
Taste
         the
                  freedom.

A drop of still in my avalanche day.

Then a faint whimper from upstairs
echoes through my body.

And I see my coffee.

Already it looks cold and old,
abused from endless reheatings.

Waiting for Daddy

Ticktock, ticktock,
That's how the clock goes.
For him, you grow up too fast;
For me, each day is too slow!

16

Unrelenting

Wipe him
Change him
Though life's at stake
in a devastating quake
Wipe him
Change him

Feed him
Bathe him
Though death appears
or bombers near
Feed him
Bathe him

Soothe him
Tickle him
Though all is dire
and lost in fire
Soothe him
Tickle him

The Darkness Within

Mommy, it's dark in there.

    Shh, I'm trying to read.
    Give me a minute.
    There is nothing to be scared of.

Mommy, it's *dark* in there.

    What are you afraid of?
    You don't know what lurks nearby.
    I don't *let* you know.

Mommy, it's *dark* in there.

    You've never seen my dreams
shackled and beaten,
    You've never heard this crated bitch
howl,
    You've never smelled my mind, now
rotten.

Mommy, it's dark in there!

    You can't give me one goddamn
minute?
    Haven't I given enough?
    What the hell do you want now?

I want . . . (sob) I want you.

Go to Sleep

"Go to sleep."
Defiant eyes stay open.
"Go to sleep."
My hunger emerges, my anger surges.

Her eyes wide,
mine hot, and yes, wide,
spitting wildfire.

Lash out, get out, thrash out,
push out, shout, "Go to sleep!"
        A shriek and sobs of snotty tears.

Fear.
Scared of what? Me.

Swallow hard. Contain it. Control me.
Breathe.
Put hunger aside. Make anger subside.
Breathe.

Never again,
I promise.
I can be better
than
me.

Ice Cream

Expressions of Playfulness

Pumpkin Hunter

Gotta wash your hands if they're dirty,
Gotta dry your hands when they're wet.
Can't let your shoes get muddy,
Or I will get upset.

But today at the farm
Where the pumpkins grow,
You in your wagon,
Daddy gives you a tow.

Scouring the ground for your prize,
This hunter is ready to jump,
But you wait for the perfect pumpkin
With the perfect little stump.

Finally, you spot the best ones,
Caked in mud and dirt.
Howling a hearty war cry,
Your body tensed and alert.

Now is your chance to get filthy,
You'll try your best to get wet,
Certainly you'll end up muddy,
To bring me the bestest pumpkin yet!

Ode to a Dirty Diaper

Such perfume was never known.
No one was ever more alone
Than when it would appear.
The stench would cause great fear.

Who will take this loathesome task?
Who has thought to bring a mask?
A head turns away,
Nothing more to say.

The eyes move quickly to the ground,
The babe will soon be passed around.
The bulge is large and dark,
This bullet's met its mark.

All hear a shockingly noisy feat.
They form a hastily planned retreat.
One person stands apart,
Unflinching of the fart.

The mother comes to baby's aid,
Of steel her nerves and nose are made.

Her smile shocks the room;
They've expected her to swoon.

Instead the mother checks inside
And says with maternal pride,
"I couldn't be more elated,
She's been so constipated."

My Little Sponge

You soak up words I say,
You soak up things I do.
You take in how I feel,
And then you feel it too.

You absorb the way I cook,
You absorb the way I dress.
You are certainly my little sponge,
So how can you make such a mess?

A Summer Day's Mischief

Dry, hot sun
beats down, hard,
heat radiating
from plants in the yard.

Wishing for a cool pool
with a shady tree,
but nothing is here
except you and me.

Your face is streaked
with sweaty lines of salt,
your water bottle tossed
in severe drought.

But then, a tug of mischief
on your lips,
a determined look,
hands on your hips.

Quick like a sand crab
on the beach,
you scurry away,
far out of reach.

Dropping your drawers
and pulling off your shirt,
you toss them carelessly
into the dirt.

Suddenly a yellow jacket
is interested in you,
and you have no clothes,
not even a shoe!

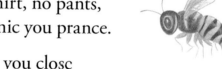

No shirt, no pants,
in panic you prance.

I pull you close
and wave it away.

"Put on your clothes,"
I sternly say.

"But it's *so hot*,"
you whine, my naked tot.

He's right, I think,
as I glance around

And then toss *my* shirt
onto the ground.

Picky Eater

I give you carrots, grapes, and mango pulp,
Curried peas,
But not a gulp.

I offer chocolate milk with cookies to dip,
Vegetable juice,
But not a sip.

Maybe pizza with onions, just a taste?
Homemade flan—
It's all a waste.

Never a bite or chew,
Never a chomp or nibble,
Until you see the doggie's food
Under the kitchen table!

Cheese

Expressions of Time Passing

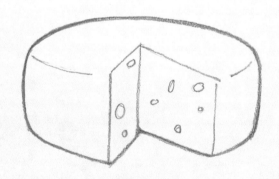

30

Fleeting

Midnight feedings,
gigglEs erupt,
triMming toenails,
jumping Off the bed.
fiRst words,
spIt-up,
rattlEs,
fingerS painted red.

watercOlors,
licking Frosting.

melted Crayons,
batHtime before bed.
dIapers,
spilled miLk,
birthDays,
owwies on the Head.
going dOwnhill on a sled.
bank accOunts thinner than thread.
the many, many, "i love yous" we have saiD.

Out with the Old

Little squares of pink and green,
Here's a favorite—aquamarine.
Once you were treasured,
Quickly washed and dried,
To keep our household clean.

You wiped noses and mopped spit-up,
You soaked milk from clumsy cups,
And once even made the bleeding stop.
But now, with you stacked on top,
This donation box is all filled up.

Mile by Mile

Uh-oh,
Cereal on the floor.
Uh-oh,
Teach, then teach some more.

Ding-dong,
Go along when stranger's at the door.
Ding-dong,
Must be strong when you can't be sure.

Bye-bye,
Always try, encourage him to soar.
Bye-bye,
Never lie and never shut the door.

33

Connected

You grew inside
Me.
You were a part of
Me.
Not me. Us.

The thick twisted rope of life,
Cut to let your life be free of me.
Naive notion.

We'll never be free.
Not you. Not me. Us.

I tasted
The sweet strawberry of your first kiss.

The thrill of your first car
Raced my heart too.

When you are fired from your job,
When on your knees you sob,

Talk to me.
You're never alone
Because

I feel it too.

Mother's Tears

The day you opened your eyes
And saw us, a new world waiting for you,
I cried
With relief and exhaustion.

One day, you will open your eyes
And see it, adventure coaxing you away.
And I will cry
With pride and fear.

Someday, I will open my eyes
And see you, a queen in your cloud castle.
And I will only cry
With joy (I promise).

Printed in the United States
By Bookmasters